INSIDE MY PRISON OF DARKNESS

INSIDE MY PRISON
OF DARKNESS

UNDERSTANDING POST-TRAUMATIC STRESS DISORDER

JOSEPH SCHILLACI

iUniverse, Inc.
Bloomington

Inside My Prison of Darkness
Understanding Post-Traumatic Stress Disorder

iUniverse books may be ordered through booksellers or by contacting:

iUniverse
1663 Liberty Drive
Bloomington, IN 47403
www.iuniverse.com
1-800-Authors (1-800-288-4677)

Because of the dynamic nature of the Internet, any web addresses or links contained in this book may have changed since publication and may no longer be valid. The views expressed in this work are solely those of the author and do not necessarily reflect the views of the publisher, and the publisher hereby disclaims any responsibility for them.

Any people depicted in stock imagery provided by Thinkstock are models, and such images are being used for illustrative purposes only.

Certain stock imagery © Thinkstock.

ISBN: 978-0-595-43838-9 (sc)
ISBN: 978-0-595-88163-5 (e)

Printed in the United States of America

iUniverse rev. date: 07/12/2012

Dedication

This book is dedicated to the people who mean the most to me, the people who saved not only my life but also my spirit.

When my world came to an end on that dreadful night and everything crumbled around me, it wasn't the priest, therapist, friends, or coworkers who picked up the pieces. Or endured the horror that was about to come.

It was my family.

To my soul mate, Evelyn, and children, Perry, Ashley, and Tiffany.

"Daddy's back and here to stay."

Special Thanks

To Aaron East for his amazing heart that came through the lens of his camera, which helped bring this book to life with his incredible pictures.

•

I would also like to thank Deputy Sheriff Rebecca Dyer for giving me motivation to move forward, not only on the book, but also on sharing my life and experiences all over our majestic country.

•

To the Miami Police Department, and its proud men and women who serve, which gave me the experiences to share.

About the Author

An Italian-born man, Joe Schillaci was raised by a mother who believed that life was simply an appreciation and love for people. His father, a true believer, who taught him that life was nothing more than family. When asked what his passions are in life, Joe remarks, "People." He explains, "Some people love clothes, jewelry, fast cars, homes, sports, or traveling. My love for life is simply *people*."

At the age of six, Joe traveled from the very cold climate of Buffalo, New York, to sunny South Florida with his mother, who had recently married a man who wanted to give his new family a fresh start on life. So, Joe, along with his mother and three younger siblings, Jamie, Steven, and Tommy all moved with the man, who had little in his pocket but great aspirations for his new family. Soon he made a life for his family in a modest three bedroom home, just minutes from majestic downtown Miami, Florida.

Joe, who is known by many as Timmy, was given this nickname by his mother due to his golden curly hair that resembled the character Tiny Tim. One of Joe's greatest lessons in life came at the age of six, as he stood in the airport with his mother. Here he would watch the amazing monsters in the sky take off and land. One day, his mother said these words: "Timmy, don't just watch the planes, watch the people getting off and going on them." She encouraged him to see how different they all were, from all over the world, and to appreciate how this made them special. From that moment on, Joe has been studying people and his love for them.

On September 22, 1991, Joe's world and his passion for life crumbled as everything he lived for and stood by shattered. On a red moon night as a police officer for the City of Miami, he would be forced to take the life of a young teenager. Joe would spend years living in darkness, or what he describes as a "living death," because of his anguish of that night. Not until he learned *forgiveness*—the one thing his late mother, and inspiration for writing this book, taught him—will he be driven from the dungeons of hell and back into the light of love.

Inside My Prison of Darkness: Understanding Post-Traumatic Stress Disorder

For those of you who are open-minded, patient, and—more importantly—open-hearted, this book will take you on a journey deep into the core of my heart. It is a heart that was lost to darkness—a darkness that can't be described.

My name is Joseph Schillaci, and I'm an Italian man who was born in Buffalo, New York, in 1961. My father, who I lost to cancer in June 2011, and I left in 1968 to travel to and live in sunny South Florida. He picked up his family of six and moved my mother—the inspiration to make a difference in any way I can—just outside one of the most amazing cities in the world, majestic Miami.

I became a police officer in 1983 and am currently assigned to the Tactical Operations Section of the City of Miami Police Department as a Deputy Commander. I just started my twenty-ninth year of service, and I write that with tremendous pride, considering just how fortunate I have been.

For those who read this book and become close-minded because they believe that PTSD is only associated with war veterans, I don't ask you to read on; I beg you. Like so many others before me, I always believed that if I opened up my true emotions and let a therapist or somebody know how I was really feeling, I would lose my livelihood. I would lose it because I would be taken off the streets and be put behind a desk or, even worse, institutionalized. All of that couldn't be further from the truth.

If the truth must be told, had I not opened up and spoken of my event, I wouldn't have lost my livelihood—I would have lost my life. I am speaking about my physical life—not my spiritual or emotional life that was already lost.

According to the National Institute of Mental Health, in 2007 suicides were the tenth leading cause of death in the United States. They accounted for 34,598 deaths in our country.

Almost twenty-nine years ago, I sat in my academy classroom as a young, cocky Italian kid from New York. I couldn't wait for our first instructions. I sat in the first seat of the first row. A crazy man stormed into the room and screamed, "Before your careers are over, two of you will die!" The crazy man, who was a training advisor, never said how we would die—just that we would die.

For those of you who might be losing a little patience with me, please tighten up your bootstraps as I do something police officers are not accustomed to and strip myself. No, I don't mean take my clothes off—I mean become extremely vulnerable.

If I can help just one person—not just one police officer, but one person who reads this—then showing you my spirit or vulnerability will be worth it. Please let me warn you that this manual will be graphic, funny, and extremely emotional.

This manual will teach you how to manage stress—the silent killer—on a daily basis. I assure you if you don't manage it, it will manage you. It will most certainly manifest itself into heart disease, cancer, chest pains, heart palpitations, liver disease, lung ailments, and—yes, once again—suicide.

You owe it to yourself and—just as importantly—your family to learn from it, communicate, and teach others about it.

I dedicate this book to the people who made it all happen for me, the real heroes in this event: my family. I would also like to give thanks to my department for all of their support over the years in allowing me to be who I am—and not what I am. It will make sense in the end; sit back and enjoy.

Chapter One

The Event

What is post-traumatic stress disorder? I will walk you through my experience involving a police shooting and describe what my family and I went through, before, during, and after. I will attempt to achieve what I had hoped someone would have done for me twenty years ago.

I swore if I survived my incident emotionally and physically that it would be my crusade in life to educate not only police officers, but people from all walks of life about the physical and emotional effects of violence.

MayoClinic.com describes PTSD in the following way:

> Post-traumatic stress disorder (PTSD) is a type of anxiety disorder that's triggered by a traumatic event. You can develop post-traumatic stress disorder when you experience or witness an event that causes intense fear, helplessness, or horror.

Many people who are involved in traumatic events have a brief period of difficulty adjusting and coping. However, with time and healthy coping methods, such traumatic reactions usually get better. In some cases, though, the symptoms can get worse or last for months or even years. Sometimes they may completely disrupt your life. In these cases, you may have post-traumatic stress disorder.

I will begin by introducing you to my wife, Evelyn, and the events in her life that contributed to her very own bouts with PTSD. In order to understand our challenges with PTSD, you need to understand my wife and myself a little better. Let me take you back in time so you can understand why she is so important to me. My wife was born from her mother's womb straight into a social worker's hands. She never touched, saw, or knew her mother, siblings, or family. She only knew what the inside of an orphanage looked like and several foster homes. What she can remember of being a young girl isn't pretty, but it must be told.

She remembers being rushed in the middle of the night from one foster home to another, but she couldn't understand why she couldn't take her baby doll. The fact of the matter is that she wasn't able to have any toys as a little girl because she didn't stay anywhere long enough to collect them. The one thing she was able to keep was a sad clown—and that's how she identified herself.

From being beaten and tied to an old furnace in a dark, damp basement, to being raped as a little girl, she endured it all physically. Her soul was lost. A little innocent girl could only identify her life as a sad, lonely clown.

Her foster brothers would bully her into running back and forth across the driveway while they used her as target practice and threw ice balls at her, striking her in the face and breaking her glasses. Did they get punished for their evil acts? No, but Evelyn did for having broken glasses. Her foster mother—who only used Evelyn as a paycheck from the government—would tape her glasses up and send her to school looking like the orphan that she was.

When she couldn't stand being tortured anymore and was smart enough to understand, she ran away to Florida from the dungeon that had imprisoned her on Long Island.

Life didn't get much easier. At age 18—on the streets of Miami—an older man befriended her and took advantage of her weakness. Soon after her arrival, she became pregnant and was living on a small boat off of Biscayne Bay.

After giving birth to her first child Perry, she befriended a lady who ran foster homes for the physically and mentally challenged and moved in with her so she could work and provide for her baby.

I could go on and on, but I think you get the picture. When I met and fell in love with my sole purpose for breathing, I knew life would be different for both of us. I knew if our marriage was going to last, I would have to get her to open up. She was so quiet and closed in from her experiences, but she fell in love with this fun-loving, passionate, and crazy kid from right outside of Miami. I grew up in a very affectionate and loving family—a love she never experienced.

To give you a glimpse into our past, I will share one of the happier moments in our lives. On Evelyn's birthday, I was going to give her a happy clown for the first time in her life. I dressed up as a happy clown, and I climbed inside a refrigerator box that was wrapped in birthday paper and contained one hundred balloons. I told Evelyn that a friend of mine had been involved in a serious car accident and that I had to go to Ohio on her birthday but my family would be there to celebrate it with her. She cried like a lost girl, but she understood.

After climbing into the box, I was delivered by a friend who was dressed like a delivery man. He pulled me off his truck and wheeled me into the house. "Special delivery for Evelyn Roman!" the delivery man said.

Just as my family was escorting her from a rear room, I jumped out of the box and scared the living mess out of her. I was dressed like a clown with a giant box of Cracker Jacks. She knew it was me, but she didn't know what to make of the moment.

She stood there, stunned and confused, my family kept screaming at her to eat the Cracker Jacks. You romantic hearts out there know what's at the bottom of the Cracker Jacks. Evelyn was eating so slowly that my family was taking handfuls to get to the bottom of the box. As she pulled the ring from the box, I knelt at her knees and said, "Will you marry me?" With tears streaming down her face, she replied, "Yes."

If you think that was crazy, wait until I tell you how we spent our first anniversary.

I thought our first anniversary should be just as special as my proposal, so I decided to do another crazy prank. I told her that I was a rookie cop and my department wouldn't let me off of work to celebrate. She cried like a little girl again as I drove away from our house with my uniform tightly pressed around my body.

Now this is our secret—please don't tell my chief. I pulled my car into an alley and took all of my clothes off. I put on a bright yellow raincoat with orange lettering on the back that said "Miami Police." I drove back to the house with a huge bottle of champagne and a blue ribbon—blue was her favorite color—and my birthday suit.

I knocked on the front door. When she opened it, I opened my raincoat and exposed my birthday suit. I said, "Happy anniversary, baby." She slammed the front door and I had to quickly move my hips backward from the door, cutting off the ribbon that was wrapped—well, I'll leave that up to your imagination.

Now, fast-forwarding eight years later, she decided she was going to pay me back and showed up unexpectedly at the station to take me out to a nice dinner in Miami. As she approached the front desk to page me, she heard my voice over the police radio trying to buy marijuana from a young kid. Instead of getting the surprise of my life from my wife, I got it from the kid. As the deal was going down, the kid pulled a gun and put it right between my eyes. Thinking I was Superman, I reached for my gun, and he responded by saying, "I know you are going for your gun. If you move, I'll blow you and your partner's head off."

As I screamed for my life into the police radio, unbeknownst to me, my wife also heard the horror from inside the police station. She screamed hysterically, "That's my husband. That's my husband!" And then there was dead silence on the radio as I tried to stay alive. During that silence, the 15 had eyes of cold blooded ice as he pointed the gun directly at my head as I sat in the driver's seat of an open jeep. I slowly tried to drive away in fear of making a sudden movement and being shot. Moments later, I observed him run between some houses as he disappeared into the darkness. We set up a perimeter, but it was too late, he was gone.

Evelyn was rushed into a rear office at the police station, waiting for word, when I came back on the radio and told my backup officers that I was all right and not to tell my wife anything because she was expecting me home early. Needless to say, I had no idea she had heard the horror and thankfully nobody was physically hurt that day. Although, emotionally, it effected both of us.

Getting treatment as soon as possible after post-traumatic stress disorder symptoms develop may prevent PTSD from becoming a long-term condition.

The event begins on September 22, 1991. I was training a new narcotics detective in the old "Jump Out Squad." At 7:22 p.m. we received an assignment to buy four bags of marijuana for twenty dollars from a very well-known hot spot in the city, 1606 NW 58th Terrace, or Liberty City, Miami. The area was known for street drug sales and violent robberies. As a matter of fact, we were just starting to experience a rash of tourist robberies in Miami, and a great deal of them were in the Liberty City area.

We had already experienced some incidents that day with young males running from us with guns. I asked my "eyeball," or "spotter," to move closer to the location where we were buying. The spotter's responsibility was to watch our backs; if anything went wrong, he'd report it to the backup officers.

On this day, my partner, Curtis Hoosier, a young black narcotics detective, was the driver. Since he was the rookie, he was the driver. We were driving a blue 1990 Chevrolet Prism. Just as we made the turn onto NW Seventeenth Avenue and Fifty-Eighth Terrace, four young black males ran up to the car and stopped us in the middle of the street.

They yelled, "Pull over, five-o" (street slang for police in the area). Apparently their counter-surveillance spotted our tactical officers setting up in the area to do the takedown or arrest after the narcotics purchase was made. I had asked the teams to move up closer because I had a bad feeling about doing the undercover operation.

Just as we made the turn, I noticed a bright red ball that looked like the sun directly in front of me. I was confused because, as a former Boy Scout, I didn't understand why the sun was setting to the east when it sets to the west. There are old Indian myths about the red moon meaning death. What I thought was the sun was actually a full red moon.

After being told to pull over, Curtis moved the car to the shoulder directly in front of two three-story public housing buildings.

The scene consisted of several single-family homes, apartment buildings, and small businesses. Just so you don't get the wrong idea—it isn't the ghetto, as some people would describe it. It's an area where people—like anybody else—are just trying to raise their children. Unfortunately, some of these areas are impoverished and have their share of violence. This violence was a way of life and had been passed down from generation to generation.

As we pulled the car over next to a large steel fence surrounding the apartment buildings, four young men approached. They were all yelling and asking us what we wanted. I told them we wanted four nickel bags of weed, or street slang for twenty dollars of marijuana. One of the four then asked me for the money so he could go get the weed.I told him that I didn't want to give him the money without the weed because, weeks earlier, on the same block a young kid put a gun to our heads and threatened to kill us.

This is the scene of the shooting.

He then said, "Don't worry; I'll go get the weed." Three of the four subjects' then ran to the corner store.

Throughout this story, I say, "This is a teachable moment." What I mean is that it's time for me to take a moment and explain in detail exactly what something means because I want to leave something for younger officers who might read this.

I have traveled all over the country in the last five years, speaking to over 150,000 children and adults about my experiences. I have voiced a concern that adults and veterans need to leave our legacies with the younger ones. When I was coming up through the ranks, the veterans—not the books—taught me how to survive. Over the last ten years, I have seen a decline in mentoring the younger kids or officers. It is our responsibility to keep them safe.

I talk about how the hairs on the back of your neck stand up when there is danger on the horizon. Your inner voice is telling you this. For years, I thought this was psychological, but the more I read or thought, the more I learned about my body and brain.

I was shocked to read that the inner voice was actually my brain physically sending my body signals to get ready to defend itself (the flight-or-fight response).

Doctor Neil F. Neimark at the Mind/Body Education Center describes the fight-or-flight response:

> This fundamental physiologic response forms the foundation of modern day stress medicine. The "fight-or-flight response" is our body's primitive, automatic, inborn response that prepares the body to "fight" or "flee" from perceived attack, harm, or threat to our survival.

This is the response that ultimately saved my life. The three subjects returned from the store, but they were walking very slowly. The subject in the middle (nineteen-year-old Duran Gordon) had his hand over his waistband to conceal an object. The hairs on the back of my neck stood up as my flight-or-fight response was activated. I immediately turned to Curtis and yelled, "Robbery!"

At the same time, Duran ran around to Curtis's side of the car, pulled a chrome-plated semiautomatic handgun, and began to beat Curtis on the head with it, so I thought. It looked as if Duran was pistol whipping Curtis, and I thought If I didn't do anything he would have seriously injured or even killed him.

In actuality Duran had pulled the trigger five times in an attempt to assassinate Curtis. I didn't learn this until many years later from reading the case file.

This was the gun Duran Gordon used.

As I exited the front passenger's door and crawled behind the rear of the car, I could hear Curtis begging for his life. "That's all I have! That's all I have!"

This is where I exited my car.

Curtis had already given Duran the buy money (money used to buy the marijuana) and his watch. However, Duran wanted more, including Curtis's life.

Duran yelled, "Give me your wallet." Curtis couldn't because he was a rookie and hadn't thought to buy an undercover dummy wallet. He only had his police-issued wallet with his badge and identification. I stood up and took the combat position (muscle memory) that I had been taught so many times over so many years.

Muscle Memory: When you train your muscle to move and react over and over again, you instill muscle memory. I had trained on the firing range for ten straight years and taught my brain and body to move a certain way when I came under fire. I didn't have to even think about what I was doing when I had to engage in combat; my body and brain just naturally reacted to what I was facing. This is why I tell people to take their training seriously because they will revert back to it.

Things began to slow down, and flashes of light like a movie went through my mind. I screamed, "Police!" to distract Duran, and he turned in my direction. I then began to experience tunnel vision.

I took a combat position from the left corner panel of the car.

Wikipedia describes tunnel vision (also known as "Kalnienk vision") as "the loss of peripheral vision with retention of central vision, resulting in a constricted circular tunnel-like field of vision."

Wikipedia describes some medical/biological causes:

- extreme fear or distress
- periods of high adrenaline production, such as an intense physical fight

As I stood up in my shooting stance, I clearly saw my first round strike Duran's neck. I could see it erupt. Instead of him falling, he continued to turn in my direction, pointing the gun at me. I fired my second round, and it struck him in his right shoulder, causing the round to get lodged underneath his armpit.

Still turning, I fired my third round, and it struck him on the right side of his chest. My eyes were so focused that it felt as if he were centimeters from me when he was actually about seven feet away. Adding more confusion to my mind that was still trying to compute what was happening, I saw Duran's body float to the ground. As the following events occurred, my mind began to see and believe things that weren't actually happening. Although, at the time, and even sometimes today, they were very, very real to me. This is typical in a combat stress situation or a situation where you feel your life is in jeopardy and everything is slowing down. The event felt like it took hours, but it only took seconds.

I ran up on Duran, keeping my gun trained on the threat. To my horror, I saw an eruption of blood flow from his mouth. Even while he was on the ground, he still had the gun in his hand and could have used it. This is why you never take your gun off of a threat.

After Duran was shot, he fell to the ground.

I still smell and taste his blood in my mouth. Before I could gather my thoughts, a barrage of gunfire came at me, and I dove through the open window of the driver's door and over my dead partner's body.

During my presentations—and over the last five years—I have told people that I thought my first round went through Duran's neck and struck my partner in his head. However, when my first round went off, Curtis' head slumped forward into the steering wheel, but he wasn't shot. He thought he was shot because the barrel of Duran's gun was pressed against his head. When I fired my first round, Curtis thought it was the projectile coming out of the barrel of the gun.

After diving through the open window over Curtis's limp body, I hit the gearshift with such force that the sharp pain had me believing I took my first round in my solar plexus. I landed on the floorboard, and I can still hear the gasping sounds. I tried my hardest to reinflate my lungs with oxygen.

I was in a fetal position on the floorboard. I realized that I was gasping so I must have still been alive. I could hear rounds striking the top of the car and knew it was a matter of seconds before I got struck again. I needed to get better cover and get behind the engine block. I decided to crawl out of the car and get underneath it.

This is where I laid on the floorboard of the car.

Holding my stomach with one hand and crawling out of the passenger's side with the other, I landed on the ground. As soon as my body hit the ground, dozens of rounds hit all around my body. The asphalt exploded, and I thought I was struck several more times.

The rounds never stopped coming; I believed that I was dying. I had such a profound sense of hopelessness and couldn't stand the thought of not seeing my family again. I remembered looking underneath the car at Duran on the other side. Thinking that it could be the last thing in life that I would see, I gave up the fight.

Shooter number one was positioned behind the dumpster.

*Shooter number two was on the second floor
landing of the apartment building.*

That's right. I broke the golden rule and gave up the fight. I shot and killed a young kid. At the time, thought I had shot and killed my partner—and I was shot and dying. There was no hope. I wanted to go home and knew I couldn't. It was time to say good-bye to my family. I could hear my heart slowing down as it beat tightly against my chest.

The noise of gunfire, the horrific screams, officers yelling, "Officer down on the street, officer down on the street," and the police sirens all faded. I closed my eyes and believed I was seeing my three-year-old Ashley with her marble-blue eyes looking down at me with an enormous smile. I said, "You're too young to understand why Daddy's not coming home, but when you are lonely and want to speak to me, look into the bright sky and I'll be listening."

Then my six-year-old Tiffany knelt down next to Ashley and me. I said, "Hey, sweetheart, Ashley will not understand, but you will. Be there for her. When you want to see me, look into the clouds and I'll be there. Stand still and feel a cool breeze wash across your face; it will be my lips on your cheeks."

Then my son wrapped his arms around his baby sisters. I said, "You're the man of the house. Your mother will not be able to handle this. This family is yours to raise." How do you tell a thirteen-year-old to be the man of the house? I just didn't know what else to say besides what I was feeling.

I didn't get a chance to talk to my wife, who I had saved for last. Just as she came into vision, rounds began exploding all around me. I felt a pull at my shirt. I was being dragged to the back of the car by Officer Renae Landa and Officer Alejandro Oliva. Gunfire erupted all around them.

I screamed, "I'm shot! I'm shot!" Officer Rolando Jacobo, Officer Alex Macias, and Officer Angel Lopez shielded my body while Landa and Oliva checked to see where the bullet holes were to administer first aid. Renae said, "No you're not. You have to fight. Get up and fight." At the same time, they were taking gunfire from the south. While risking his life and trying to administer first aid, Officer Oliva was taking on gunfire. He immediately unholstered his gun, fired several rounds to drive back the shooter, reholstered, and went back to giving me first aid. With their lives in peril, the officers never left my side.

I screamed behind the car I'm shot! I'm shot!

As I stood up, over 107 rounds of gunfire kept coming at us in the firefight. I then witnessed a mother pushing her hysterically crying baby into the street. Again, I believed my partner was dead. I knew I had just killed a young kid, and now this baby was in harm's way, caught between Duran's friends and my backup officers.

I turned my attention away from the shots and pointed my gun at the mother's face. I said, "I can't come out from my cover. Get your baby or I'll shoot you."

Just as I was getting ready to squeeze off a round, she grabbed her child and ran to safety. When she gave us a sworn, taped statement, she said that she had used her child as a shield because she thought we would stop shooting.

A mother pushed her two year old baby into the street between two parked cars across the street from where the shooting happened.

Teachable Moment:

As a police officer, you receive the best of the best training. You are a well-oiled machine ready to lay your life on the line. However, there are some things that are better trained.

We live by every law in the book—Supreme Court law, state law, city law, moral and ethical law—but the person who is trying to take you away from your family lives by only one law and that is to survive.

These young men took up a preplanned, strategic position that was practiced like any SWAT team as they fired upon us. We know this for a fact because we found their journals and charts and matched up their positions to the charts that had been practiced long before they met us.

As quickly as it started, it ended. I stood in the middle of the street with a cloud of smoke that filled the air and burned my eyes. My legs were shaking. I could barely feel them or stand up when I saw Officer Sherlie Harvard running up to me. She reached around me and kept me from collapsing. She walked me over to a car that was roped off with crime scene tape.

I said, "I killed a young boy. I killed a young boy."

She said, "No, Joey. You saved your partner's life." I was too confused to understand. She sat me in the passenger seat of the car and walked away.

To add more confusion to mayhem, I saw Curtis—or his ghost—out of the corner of my eye in the driver's seat. He looked just as confused as I was. I said, "Curtis, what are you doing here? I killed you."

He said, "No, you didn't—and you saved my life." He put his head down in his lap, and we never spoke about it again—at least not for sixteen years.

Teachable Moment:

At the beginning of all my presentations, I tell the audience that most—if not all—will recover from a traumatic experience if they just talk about it and do not let it develop into something worse. This is called talk therapy, and most victims of post-traumatic stress will recover through talk therapy. In most cases, they will not even develop the disorder. One of the myths that I learned through the experience is that it might not be one big event like a shooting, a hurricane, or a rape.

We are learning that children who become victims of bullying suffer from post-traumatic stress—even playing violent video games can bring it on. This doesn't just pertain to children; bullying in the workplace is a serious problem that can escalate into physical violence.

Every single one of us will experience and recover from a traumatic event in our own unique way. I recall as I was sitting in the car with the door wide open, looking at Curtis, and the hundred or so onlookers who had gathered around the crime scene.

They were pointing at me saying, "You shot and killed that boy—and now we're going to your house to kill your family."

They weren't really saying that at all—it was my mind playing tricks on me, which is common after a traumatic event. In all actuality, they were very supportive of me and came forward as witnesses to the shooting.

Chapter Two

The Aftermath

At this point in the book or presentation, I would like to say that I lived happily ever after—but that wasn't the case at all. This is the point where the book really begins. Sit back and tighten up your bootstraps because this will get extremely emotional.

There were so many nights, days, weeks, months, and years that I wished I'd stayed on that bloody street. I would have been better off, or at least my family would have been.

For two years, I suffered from isolation, depression, confusion, loneliness, and darkness. I literally became a prisoner of darkness, trapped with no way out. My coworkers would say, "You walked and looked like a zombie." When I asked them why they didn't say anything to me, they would reply, "We were afraid of sending you off the edge." This is another myth with PTSD—not asking me how I was or getting me to talk about the event was causing more damage—damage that would soon drive me to the edge.

Imagine my wife and I watching a cop show and seeing a police officer get shot in the neck. I spontaneously jumped to my feet and began running through the house with her chasing me. I screamed, "Curtis, I'm shot, I'm shot!" as I was holding my neck. She had to dive on top of me. As she shook me, she said, "Honey, you're all right. You're safe; you're at home."

Ashley, my three-year-old, was crying as she stood over us. She said, "Mommy, what's wrong with Daddy? What's wrong with Daddy?"

"Daddy's okay. Go in the other room."

What I had experienced at that moment was a flashback, a common symptom of PTSD. I actually went back into the scene and had seen myself shot. Nobody ever taught me this; I had to learn it the hard way.

Flashback
By Matthew Tull, PhD, About.com Guide
Updated April 29, 2008
About.com Health's Disease and Condition content is reviewed by the
Medical Review Board

Dr. Matthew Tull, PhD, describes flashbacks as "one of the re-experiencing symptoms of PTSD. As the name implies, in a flashback, a person may feel or act as though a traumatic event is happening again.

A flashback can vary in severity. A flashback may be a temporary occurrence, and a person may maintain some connection with the present moment. On the other hand, during a flashback, a person may lose all awareness of what is going on around them, being taken completely back to their traumatic event. Similar to a dissociative episode, during a flashback, a person may also lose track of time."

At the academy, our training advisor had never told us how we would die, just that we would die. I had died not physically, but I had emotionally. There was no bringing life back to me. Daddy's singing, dancing, and playful ways were gone forever. My soul was lost and imprisoned in darkness with no light—not even a flicker.

If that wasn't bad enough, I was cutting a cucumber for salad one night. I loved to cook, so my wife didn't mind. The peels fell slowly into the sink—like Duran's body falling slowly into the street. I heard faint voices behind me. As they got louder and louder, I thought, *I shot and killed a young kid. I lost my family and friends, and I am on the verge of losing my job—and now I'm hearing voices.*

What did I have to lose? I would turn around and face my voices. When I did this, to my astonishment, it was my wife crying. She was screaming, "Why don't you talk to us? Where's my husband? Why don't you talk to us?"

I replied, "I can't bring him back."

For years, I thought it was Duran that I couldn't bring back, but it was me. I couldn't escape the darkness, and I would soon be another statistic.

That first day of the academy, we had also learned that police officers were number three on the list for most suicides in our country. Let me sadly announce that today we have forged our way to the front and are now number one. I was on the verge and knew if I didn't get help, I would be on the list.

Let me tell you two examples that best depict what I'm trying to get across. The first story is about my mentor, my god, my field training officer (FTO). Out of respect for him, I will call him Officer Mike. At the time, I thought Officer Mike was the perfect cop. He was so professional, kind, passionate, and true to society. He was everything I could have hoped to be in law enforcement.

One day, I saw Mike walking away from the police department in a zombie-like state. I said, "Man, that was me—that's what I must have looked like."

Fearing for his well-being, I approached him and said, "Mike, you don't look so good. Are you going to be all right?"

He just threw his hand up in the air to gesture that he was all right and kept walking. Instead of pushing the issue—like everybody else, I thought I was going to push him over the edge—I just turned around and walked away.

Officer Mike was going through some stuff at home and work and didn't know how to *communicate* it. Instead of getting help, he reverted to drug abuse. His abuse got so bad that he would sell and use heroin out of his police car to support his habit.

Officer Mike is currently serving a thirty-five-year sentence in prison for kidnapping his girlfriend and beating her. This was my god, my mentor, a man with not even a traffic ticket on his record. He didn't commit physical suicide—he committed emotional suicide.

The second story is about a not-so-lucky friend of mine on the force. Out of respect for him, I will refer to him as Officer D. One day, I saw Officer D walking away from the station in a zombie-like state, just like Officer Mike. I didn't want to make the same mistake that I had made with Officer Mike so I approached Officer D. I said, "What's the matter? You look bad."

He replied, "My boss gave me a reprimand."

I said, "So what? It's just paper. Wipe your toes with it and move on."

That's exactly what he did—he got into his police car and moved on. He drove straight home, put a gun to his head, squeezed the trigger in front of his wife, and ended his life in front of her. That is the tragic ending we are sometimes faced with when we fail to communicate with ourselves, and each other.

Help for me would come not from a therapist, physiologist, clergy, or shrink. Although I strongly believe in therapy and should have gone long ago, the help came from my presentations. The more I spoke to other officers, teachers, parents, and students around the country, the more I learned about myself and the event.

I am going to strip myself of my suit of armor that cops love to use for protection. In reality, it's killing us. I'm not proud about these things, but if it keeps your sanity or keeps you from doing what I did to my family, then my vulnerability is worth the risk.

The more I did the presentations, the more the participants would ask me questions only my family could answer, so I decided to bring them.

I was in a small training center outside of Miami when a police officer raised his hand and asked, "What was it like for your son?"

I said, "As a matter of fact, I invited him. He's sitting in the back of the room. Why don't you ask him?"

For you to appreciate the moment, I need to describe my son. He had never spoken in public before about his experiences when he was thirteen. He's six feet tall, bald, with tattoos covering his three hundred pound body. He is a prototypical guard for a football team.

He stood up and softly said, "It wasn't so bad for me. I understood what my dad was going through. There were times I would have to scream back at him to stop treating me like a prisoner. Now for my sisters, it was tough."

As he said that, my heart sank into my stomach because I was numb and isolated and didn't remember any of it.

Perry would say, 'We had a loft in a two-story home, and my dad filled that loft with every imaginable toy a child could have. However, when my sisters would try to come down, he would scream, 'Don't come downstairs; stay upstairs.' If the truth must be told, he created a prison for them—and didn't even know it."

I see now that I didn't want them in my world. I wanted to shield them from the evil of the outside world and was destroying them at the same time.

In 2010, I was doing a presentation in a small Midwest town when a cornbread-fed-looking guy quietly raised his hand and said, "You've told us time and time again that we should communicate with our loved ones, friends, clergy, or therapist, and I would like to know how your six-year-old daughter handled it."

I said, "She was six years old. How much could she remember?"

He then replied, "You would be surprised."

I left the presentation and got on a plane. Four hours later, I went straight home, not greeting anybody but my twenty-six-year-old daughter Tiffany. She was sitting in my living room with my family and her friends. I said, "Honey, I need to talk to you. Let's go into the garage." I had created a man cave for my kids. They had been playing pool at some pool halls and I didn't feel it was safe. I spent thousands of dollars so they could be safe with me at my house. From the loft as a six-year-old to my garage as a twenty-six-year-old, I was still trying to protect them from the outside world.

When we got into the garage, I said, "Hey, baby, I was just at a presentation and a participant wanted to know how you handled my shooting."

She said, "Daddy, you always taught me not to lie, so I am not going to lie to you."

Before I let her say one word, my stomach dropped to my feet—not even my stomach. I said, "Baby, I didn't think you were old enough to remember or understand. Was I a bad father? Did I abuse you in any way?"

She replied, "No, Daddy. You were—and still are—the best daddy ever. There was just a lot of screaming in the house—not so much at us, but you always screamed at Perry. Sometimes the screaming would get so bad that Ashley would get scared and cry. I would hide her underneath the kitchen sink so she wouldn't be so scared."

This was the same kitchen sink where I kept all of the household poisons. I warned you that this would be emotional and that I would unwrap myself and become very vulnerable. If you learn anything—and I mean anything—from this book, learn to never have this happen to the people who love you the most. What affects us directly will affect all of us indirectly.

Perry took the brunt of my hostility toward life. He was having trouble in school—and it's no wonder why. Instead of listening with my heart, I listened to him with my ears. He was trying to tell me, but I couldn't hear him—and because of it, he engaged in reckless behavior, once even getting arrested for shooting a BB gun at a moving vehicle. The BB went through the passenger's window and struck the driver. He lost control of the vehicle and ended up at the edge of a twelve-foot-deep canal. Thank God the family inside didn't sustain any serious injuries. My son, my daughter, and my wife were screaming at me physically and emotionally to find my way back to them, but I couldn't hear. I was so lost and isolated from the world and myself.

I not only isolated myself from them, but also from Curtis. For sixteen years, I would walk past him and only say hello or good-bye. This was the same man whose wife took care of my two-year-old while we were at work.

I do a lot of PTSD presentations for a very good friend. Habsi Kaba is a family and marriage therapist who teaches crisis intervention to police officers all over the country. One hand washes the other—I do presentations for her, and she allows me to cry on her shoulder. She has quietly been my pillow for five years and—thank God—hasn't billed me. As I was doing my presentation in Miami for Habsi, a young Latin officer raised his hand and said, "Lieutenant, I respect what you're doing, but you have a lot of nerve telling us to *communicate* when you haven't even talked to Curtis about the shooting."

It was like getting punched in the face and knocked to the ground. I picked myself up and said, "You're absolutely right." I went straight to the police station to meet with Curtis.

When I arrived, we met in a small office inside the community affairs section, where I was assigned at the time. I told Curtis what had just happened—and for the first time in sixteen years, he spoke about what had happened that night.

For sixteen years, I had seen the same darkness in his spirit, but I was too afraid to go back to the horrific place. However, something changed after we met. About two weeks after the meeting, I saw a man running through the parking lot of our police station. He was screaming, "Schillaci, Schillaci." He looked like a madman who had just won the lottery.

As he approached me, I realized that it was Curtis and stopped at the driver's door of my police car. As I was placing the key in the door he said, "I just got back from vacation in North Carolina. I bought a farm and want you and Evelyn to come stay with my wife and me."

I replied, "That's great, and we would love to, but I have to go home now."

"You just did the same thing that people have done to me for the past sixteen years. You listen with your ears, but not your heart. I have a cow, a horse, and a pig on my farm, and you would love it."

"Great, Curtis, but I have to go now; we'll come up and visit."

"You're still listening with your ears and not your heart."

I screamed, "I hear you. What's your problem?"

He put his head down, and his voice got slow and soft. "Do you remember Marcus, my son?"

"Yeah, how is your six-year-old?"

He picked his head up and firmly said, "He's not six. He's nineteen, and I just got back from his college graduation. I got to see my son graduate because of you, and now he works for the Philadelphia Eagles as a physical trainer. Now, are you listening with your heart? Thank you for my life."

For sixteen years, I had struggled with people telling me that I was a hero when I was just doing my job. One coworker would jump on my back as I walked into the station, try to grab my gun out of my holster, and carve a notch out of it with his buck knife. He would playfully say, "Here's my hero; give me your gun." This was the same guy who had shielded my body with his car and took a massive amount of gunfire while Renae and Alejandro were checking for bullet holes in my body.

For the first time in sixteen years, I was able to cope with people telling me I was a hero when I was just doing what God put me on this earth to do. If the truth must be told, I wasn't the hero. Aside from those brave men that ran into the street with no cover to save me, I know who the real heroes are.

In 2010, I was asked to travel to Cleveland and give a keynote speech at a police memorial. I told the organizer that I would do it if he would allow me to honor the living and not just our fallen heroes. He paused as he tried to gather his thoughts, and without preparing the speech, I told him what I was going to say. He told me that I shouldn't do the speech; I had to do the speech.

In May 2010, I gave the speech in front of three thousand police officers and their families from the Cleveland Peace Officers Association:

As the sun was setting on a humid September evening and in the span of a few seconds that felt like a lifetime, I shot and killed a young teen after he put a gun to my partner's head and squeezed the trigger five times.

After taking his life, and unbeknownst to me, his comrade street soldiers took up preplanned combat strategic positions, and 107 rounds were fired as I gazed into the lifeless body of this kid that I had killed.

When I dove for cover, I was struck in the abdomen and gasped for air. Thinking I was struck several more times and dying, I broke the golden rule and gave up the fight; you see, I was tired, and it was time to go home.

For the surviving victims of loved ones tragically killed in the line of duty, it would be a privilege to be a voice for your husbands or wives. If you have ever wondered what those final moments were and never got closure, please allow me to be their voices. Did they suffer or feel pain, and what were their final thoughts?

As I lay in the street that became my tomb, I was numb and felt nothing; everything became extremely quiet and peaceful amongst the carnage. I reached a point where the only thing I felt was the enormous love for my children and beautiful wife.

The first vision that came into sight during those final moments was of my three-year-old marble-blue-eyed baby, Ashley Nichola. I said, "Hey, sweetheart, you will never understand why Daddy's not here to be with you on the playground or beach, or will never understand why Daddy's not here to kiss your pain away.

"You will never understand why Daddy's not here to see you walk into your first school or even graduate. And, yes, baby, you will never understand why Daddy's not here to walk you down the aisle and give you away.

"But you see, Ashley, Daddy is here and will always be. All you have to do is look to the sky and feel the warmth of the sun. Stand still for a moment and feel the coolness of the breeze, and, yes, baby Ash, it is Daddy every step of the way."

Then my daughter Tiffany came into sight with her little mischievous smile. I said, "Hi, sweetheart, you had me wrapped around your finger the second I laid eyes on you in the hospital, and the nurse had to catch me before my head hit the ground from the amazement of what Daddy had created. Oh yeah, with a little help from Mom, of course.

"You see, Tiffany, you are only six years old, but a little older than Ash. Like Ash, you might not understand, but be there for your sister, for she will need you more than ever.

"And like Ash, the next time you touch the softness of an innocent flower or gaze at a glorious mountain, it's me watching over you. All you have to do is believe, and I'll be there."

Yes, I saved my partner's life that dreadful night, but I wasn't the hero. You see, the real heroes are my wife and children, who endured so much and never wavered.

From being kidnapped, robbed, having a gun placed to my head, to being beaten beyond recognition, they endured it all, and never— and I mean never—gave up on me. Their love and support only fueled my spirit.

Perry never asked why Daddy wasn't home to play football, Ashley and Tiff to play Barbie. They just knew that Daddy had to make a difference. What little time I did have with them was a lifetime.

I got so tired of disrupting my wife's sleep with the four-in-the-morning phone calls; I didn't have the courage to call the night of my shooting.

I got so tired of her seeing my broken body after foot chases and beatings. One night I decided to creep into the bedroom after being released from the hospital on crunches with a broken foot, thinking I could tell her in the morning.

She would only roll over in the bed, gently kiss me, sigh in relief that I was home, and whisper, "The next time you go to the hospital and not tell me, I'll break both your feet."

Now if that wasn't bad enough, it was certainly the hell we found ourselves living in. There were days, weeks, months, and years that I wished I'd stayed on the hot asphalt that dreadful night.

My playful ways were gone—my incredible voice in the shower was silent. My smile, my soul, and spirit were dark.

In the end, the fire from hell was put out by my family's courage to withstand. Their commitment and love for me and each other drove out the darkness from my heart that truly saved my spirit.

Yes, we honor our fallen comrades, including Elria Police Officer James Kerstetter, who was shot and killed responding to a subject who had exposed himself to a child.

Yes, Officer Kerstetter unselfishly sacrificed his life, and we honor him and others before him today, but just as importantly, we honor their families.

What lessons have we learned from these acts of unselfish courage? If James were here to speak to us today, he would say, "Don't honor me—honor the people who made me and gave me light and inspiration to be who I am: my children and soul mate, the mere reason I exist.

"Honor my mother and father for giving me guidance and the foundation in life to have the courage to lay my life on the line. Honor my bothers, sister, and friends who were there when I needed a shoulder to cry on."

Ladies and gentlemen, where do we go from here? Yes, we are soldiers protecting the front lines of our country that has been plagued by violence, and, yes, it is an awesome and sometimes overwhelming responsibility, but nonetheless, it is our honor and pride to serve.

Yes it could be a thankless job with long, lonely hours, days, and nights away from our families, but we wouldn't trade them in for a moment.

While the innocent sleep, the guilty stalk, and, yes, it is we who are there side by side, fist by fist, heart by heart so society can rest.

However, in the end, we must never forget that we are still mothers, fathers, brothers, and sisters. We are aunts, uncles, and, yes, even grandparents—and what it ultimately boils down to is we are human beings who feel and cry like anybody else.

Never lose touch with who you are and not what you are. The power doesn't lie in the badge or gun; it lies in our hearts, the mere reason we chose a profession that puts us at constant danger every second of the day to make a difference in someone's life.

Not like any other profession where they go home to their refuge and take their suit of honor off to be at peace. We are reminded that our suit of honor is on every waking moment.

In conclusion, never stop believing in why you sacrifice so much; never stop believing the difference you make in people's lives every day. Even if you never see or hear them, just believe.

Ladies and gentlemen, let this day of honor remind us of what we lost, but also let it remind us of what we have. Life is precious and fleeting—live every moment of it as if it was your last.

When you put the uniform on, know it is a symbol of freedom that allows us to live in a place where we are being protected from people who prey on the weak or unexpected.

When you go home tonight, hug your children like you've never hugged them before. Kiss your husbands and wives like you've never kissed them before. And when you look at yourself in the mirror before turning the lights out, look into your eyes, reach deep into your spirit, and thank God or whatever power you choose to believe in for giving you life.

So in the end I had to learn to find myself again, and without my family, I would have been lost in that darkness forever.

What I experienced then and now didn't mean I was losing my mind, it meant that something was broken and needed to be fixed. Nobody ever taught me what I would experience during a traumatic event, and I vowed that I wouldn't make that same mistake. I vowed that I would teach and share my experiences with anybody that was willing to listen. Some of the things that I've learned along the way are the symptoms and myths of PTSD that I would like to share with you.

Chapter Three

The Symptoms

Nightmares: Nightmares will vary from time to time. You might experience some at the beginning of your event, but they will subside as the weeks, months, and years go on. Again, it is important for you to know that some people might not experience any of these symptoms or even suffer from PTSD. However, it is important to understand and recognize the symptoms if you are experiencing them.

It doesn't mean you're losing you mind—it's just your body telling you to recognize and deal with it by *communicating*. Most people will move on with their lives and don't have any problems at all, but some may have difficulties. However, with talk therapy, most will learn to live normal healthy lives. I experienced plenty of nightmares in the beginning, but they subsided when I learned to recognize and speak about them.

If I do a presentation today, I will probably have some sort of nightmare that night because I relive the event by talking about it. I understand why and move on. When I don't recognize the correlation of the nightmare or even day-mare, I have a problem.

In September 2010, I was driving home and feeling on top of the world. I had just bought my retirement home and was ready to move in within weeks. I was planning my retirement, with several speaking engagements and a new show on the horizon. I was swimming four days a week and was obsessed with the new community that I was moving into. I was happy, singing, and acting crazy as ever when I felt an enormous feeling of helplessness on top of me. It felt like the weight of the world fell right on top of me. I began to panic, not understanding what was happening, and called my wife.

I told her that I was driving home on a major highway and couldn't understand what I was experiencing. The more I spoke, the worse it got. She begged me to pull over, but I kept saying, "I can't. I have to get home."

After hearing me speak for years in front of large audiences, she had learned exactly what I was going through, and she calmed me down right away. She asked me what the date was, and I realized it was the date of my shooting. I immediately calmed down and was safely on my way home.

Depression: Depression can be one of the most common, but dangerous, signs of PTSD. This is what will cause your life to spiral downward if you don't get help. There will be days you won't want to get out of bed—and that is definitely not healthy. You'll have one good day and two bad days. You'll have one good week and then three bad days. The point is that as the days, weeks, months, and years go on, so will you—as long as you *communicate.*

I am a tremendous advocate of therapy, but recognize when suffering from depression how one drink leads to another, and when the drink isn't putting you to sleep, you go to the doctor for a sleeping aid.

In some severe cases, it is necessary, but understand that it is just masking what is really going on inside—and it is not going to help in the long run. You need to get to the core of the problem, learn from it, and move on.

In severe cases, medication may be necessary, but for most, talk therapy will lead to some normalcy.

Lack of Concentration: You will find it difficult in the beginning to stay focused. You will always be looking for answers. I began my twentieth year since the event, and I'm still looking for answers. Understand that you must stay focused for your coworkers, employers, family, and yourself.

Feelings of Isolation: I didn't even recognize that I had isolated myself from the outside world, including my family. It wasn't until years later that I was told. Understand how devastating this can be to your friends, coworkers, and family. Everything and everybody reminded me of the scene. I fought every day against feeling negative or isolated.

In some cases, you will not only isolate yourself—you will isolate your family as well. I wanted to isolate my children from the dangers of the world, but I was creating more problems than good by isolating them. Like the story of me not allowing my children to come downstairs—I didn't chain them up, but I didn't make life any easier for them by not telling them why I was so afraid for them.

Numbness: I experienced this right after the event. I thought I had been shot in the stomach because of the sharp burning pain. It felt like hot water pouring inside my belly. However, when I was on ground, I couldn't feel anything physically—just emotionally. I knew I had to have been shot multiple times, but I couldn't feel the pain. The adrenaline rushing through my body was protecting me from it.

On the other hand, it created a lot of confusion for me. When Renae and Alejandro were screaming at me that I wasn't shot, I couldn't believe them. I knew what I initially felt, but I was numb and couldn't convince myself otherwise. This is why you can never give up. I was sending my body into shock and would have certainly died from it had it not been for the guys that saved me. The wound that I sustained was a deep bruise from landing on the gearshift when I dove through the window—and it certainly wasn't life-threatening. However, mentally sending my body into shock would have certainly killed me.

In the end, it took three days to convince myself that I hadn't been shot. On the third day, I noticed a black and blue imprint of the gearshift across my stomach. For three days, I kept feeling my stomach to see if I could find the bullet. I remember working a scene where a young lady was shot. The call came in as her having a seizure. When I got to the scene, rescue placed her into the rescue unit and couldn't understand why she wasn't responding. I remembered being taught in first responders' school that some gunshot wounds get folded over by the skin, fat, and muscle and you might not find blood or a wound. This is exactly what happened to that poor girl. As it turned out, I found a small caliber casing where fire rescue picked her body up. Sure enough—she died right in front of me from internal bleeding. She had been bleeding for some time, but we didn't know it because we couldn't see the wound or any blood.

Keep in mind that I just described a physical numbness, but there is a numbness that can't be described—an emotional numbness. You don't know you're experiencing it until your family, friends, or coworkers say, "Man, you looked like a zombie." Just know that if you experience PTSD, you will experience this numbness and not know it, and this is why you have to *communicate.*

Back Flashes: I didn't experience these often, but when I did, they were hard to understand. The most memorable one I've already described; however, what I didn't describe are the flashes of light from time to time. These flashes of light were actually flashbacks of the event being slowed down like a movie in my mind. This is a normal symptom; however, left unnoticed, they can cause problems for the spirit and mind.

Anxiety: By understanding anxiety, you can truly understand post-traumatic stress and its effects on the human body and spirit. I'm not a doctor—nor do I pretend to be—but if there is one area that haunts me even today, it's anxiety. If you understand and cope with anxiety, you truly have won half the battle. In short, anxiety means trouble. It could be in the present or past, but it is trouble. It creates feelings of worry and fear and is considered to be a normal reaction to a stressor.

There are physical and emotional effects of anxiety. Physical effects include heart palpitations, tension, fatigue, nausea, chest pains, stomachaches, and headaches. The body will naturally prepare itself to deal with the physical effects by increasing blood flow to the major muscle groups—and away from the digestive system.

While studying the late Dr. Martin Luther King and his philosophies of nonviolence, I learned that what affects one directly will affect all of us indirectly. In other words, if your child breaks a leg, you will definitely feel his or her emotional pain. I can think of no better example than my wife.

In addition to dealing with the anxiety of being an orphan most of her life, she certainly had her share of anxiety over my job and the fear of her soul mate not coming home every day. If that wasn't enough, it would have been the beatings I took or the kidnapping earlier in the year at another undercover operation. If the kidnapping didn't put her over the edge, then it would have been hearing me scream when the fifteen-year-old put a gun right between my eyes. If you haven't gotten the point now, at least be open to what I'm trying to give you.

In 2006, we experienced the first of four major stomach or intestinal surgeries that could have—and should have—cost her her life. After years of suffering from anxiety, her intestines slowed and her immune system weakened. A simple cough would land her in the hospital with pneumonia—and it was all related to anxiety. She had been diagnosed with an anxiety disorder that would go horribly wrong.

Between 2009 and 2011, more than sixteen thousand people in Florida died from prescribed medicines. On November 10, 2011, I arrived home from a normal day at work. My wife had been complaining about not feeling well for a few days. She started to fidget. She explained that the pharmacist hadn't given her all of the anti-anxiety medicine that had been prescribed weeks earlier and she was out.

I thought she was experiencing withdrawal from not being on the powerful medicine that kept her system relaxed and prevented her brain from overloading her body with hormones and adrenaline. She explained that her doctor had prescribed some new medicine, but it would take a few days for it to get into her system.

She was tired and wanted to go to bed. We went to bed at nine o'clock—and she started to shake and talk in her sleep. She would move her hands as if she were grabbing or moving things. At first, I thought it was the withdrawal, and I monitored her while she slept. For every minute of those next eight hours, her body experienced tremors and she talked in her sleep. For the entire night, she kept moving her hands and arms as if she were sleepwalking. I thought she was dreaming.

Not having experienced anything like this in my life, I figured it would take time for her body to adjust, and I waited for her to wake up. I decided to take the day off and monitor her in case I needed to take her to the hospital. When we got up, I told her that I was going to take a bike ride to burn off some stress.

As I rounded the corner to my block about an hour later, I saw her walking toward our community center. She looked extremely confused and screamed, "Where is Ashley, and why did everybody leave me?" I told her that Ashley was at work. She said, "No, she's out trick-or-treating."

I knew something was wrong because Halloween had been ten days earlier. What she had said didn't bother me as much as how she had said it—it sounded as if she were locked in the past. I asked her how old she thought Ashley, my twenty-three-year-old, was.

She replied, "Five."

I knew I needed to get her home right away because something was horribly wrong.

I got off my bike and walked her to the house. When we got inside, I sat her down on the couch.

She said, "What's wrong with the television? It won't go on."

Her hand looked as if she were holding a remote control and trying to press the power button. To my amazement and confusion, it appeared as if she were hallucinating. I immediately called the family to come over to help me out.

Her children started arriving, and they quickly noticed that their mother didn't appear to be their mother. She kept talking to people who weren't there. She was picking up objects that were not there. We talked about taking her to the hospital, but we thought that it might make the situation worse since the hospital staff did not know her history.

Things went from worse to horrific when Perry arrived. He walked in the house and went to kiss Evelyn on her cheek. She raised her arm as she sat on the couch to shake his hand and said, "Hello, Sergeant Peterson."

We closely monitored her for hours as the medicine wore off. After she came to her senses, we learned that when she had gotten the new refill of anti-anxiety medicine, she had taken five of the very powerful pills instead of two. She explained that she had been going through withdrawals so badly that she thought she could get the medicine into her system quicker if she took more than had been prescribed. Her body was desperate for the extremely addictive medicine, but instead of helping her cause, she could have killed herself.

I didn't know who Sergeant Peterson was, but I knew it wasn't Perry. After giving birth and raising him for thirty-three years, she hadn't even recognized him.

If you learn anything from this book, learn that you are not alone when you go out into the workforce to battle the evils of society. Your family is on your back—every step of the way. If you suffer, trust me, they will suffer.

The emotional effects of anxiety include feeling tense, jumpy, or apprehensive. You constantly think that danger is right around the corner. The one thing that I tell my personnel at work is to always have a mental and physical plan. Be ready for anything at any time.

It's one thing to control these emotions, but it's another when they are controlling you. When you suffer from the emotional effects of anxiety, you think the worst and become negative about everything. It's like a cancer growing in every part of your body. You will experience multiple nightmares or feel as if you are trapped in your mind.

Again, the most important part of understanding this is communicating it to someone. These are normal effects of anxiety, and you're not going crazy. If you let it get worse and do nothing about it, then you will certainly risk further harm.

Some other symptoms of anxiety include tremendous feelings of guilt, hopelessness, memory problems, trouble concentrating, and avoidance of activities that you once enjoyed.

I was raised a devout Catholic and was an altar boy. I remember an incredible feeling of guilt for taking a kid's life. As right as I was—and as much as people reminded me—it didn't soothe the pain. I was at my wit's end and didn't know where to look. I finally decided to take my self-destruction to the clergy program at the police department. We had—and still have—a group of ministers, pastors, priests, and rabbis to give us spiritual guidance after a critical incident. At the time, I chose to go to the priest because I was Catholic. I was desperate and didn't know what else to do.

He walked toward the door to exit the police department. He was in his auxiliary uniform with its dual roles of volunteer police officer and priest. With my head down and the world falling all around me, I said, "Father, I need to speak to you."

He replied, "Not now, son. I have to respond to a call."

Twenty years later, I've never told him how that moment could have cost me my life. I felt so betrayed by my faith that I couldn't believe how he could turn his back on me. However, it should also be said that that same faith saved my soul. It wasn't his fault that he had a call—and I certainly didn't tell him at the time how desperate I was. It was just another reminder for me to see how important it is to share your feelings and not let them destroy you.

Being jumpy is a big symptom. Try being a four-year-old celebrating a birthday when a balloon pops and the entire mood in the room changes from happiness to horror because Daddy thinks he's being shot at. Another time, my wife was driving into Manhattan and I heard a car backfire. I grabbed the steering wheel—at fifty miles per hour—and screamed, "They're shooting at us. They're shooting at us!"

Communication

I have saved the most important for last. If you have read this far, and have learned nothing, learn this: through communication, all is possible. The best medicine for any stress is talk therapy. After teaching the Goodwill Ambassadors for Miami, a lady walked up to me and said, "If I had taken your class a year ago, I could have saved my marriage. We never communicated with each other."

I have seen countless friends and their marriages come to an end because of a lack of communication. In the end, it was what saved my soul. When I realized that I was so close to the edge, I knew it was time to talk to a professional. Nonbelievers may say, "They're not going to understand me; they're not in my shoes." Yes, it is difficult for them to understand, but the point is to open up your prison of darkness and release the isolation, confusion, anxiety, depression, numbness, nightmares, flashbacks, and lack of communication that has you locked in darkness. You can speak it, draw it, paint it, sing it, dance it, or simply write it down—but you have to communicate it. It took me 20 years to learn from Curtis that life went on after the shooting. He didn't dwell in the horror, he just went on. He also realized that it would be a memory that would never go away, so why relive it. After 20 years, he finished his conversation by saying, "Regardless of what I've said, remember this, I wouldn't be here today if it wasn't for you." It is our responsibility to look into our souls and souls of others and listen—with your heart and not your ears. While you're listening, also look into the eyes; they are truly the path to our inner heart and soul.

We have come a long way from the days when Senior Officers would tell us if we showed our true feelings; we'd be taken off the streets. Today we have the Employees Assistance Program to assist us in any personal matters related to work or home. This is fantastic program to help us communicate.

We also have the Clergy and Crisis Programs to assist us as well.

However, even with a stronger understanding about PTSD, we still have officers afraid of sharing their feelings in fear of being labeled. Some departments are still living in the stone age, taking officers off the streets until they get help.

Some have gone to the extreme of taking the officer's gun and their identity in fear of them committing suicide, instead of getting them counseling.

Myths about PTSD

Experts have written countless articles about the myths of PTSD—and most of them say pretty much the same things.

- "If I suffer from PTSD, people will think I'm crazy."

    PTSD is as much physical as it is psychological. Not getting the help for the disorder can certainly make you feel as if you are going crazy, but talking to someone can make all the difference.

- "If I suffer from a traumatic event, I will suffer from PTSD."

This is not necessarily true. Just because you feel guilt, anxiety, fear, or anger, you won't necessarily develop PTSD. With just a little talk therapy at the onset, most people overcome the event and go on to live healthy lives. If any of these symptoms persist for more than a month, there is a strong possibility that you are suffering from PTSD—and getting professional help is a must.

- "If loved ones or friends are suffering from PTSD and I ask them if they're all right or if they want to hurt themselves, it will push them over the edge."

If I had been a little more persistent with Officer Mike, he might have not become a junkie. If I had been a little more persistent, Officer D might have not become a name on a tomb. I have spoken to tens of thousands of people over the last five years about communicating with each other. I tell them that approximately 75 percent of language is body language. That leaves a very small percentage of language that is actually verbal. With that being said, you have to listen to emotions as much as the language we speak. When people are hurting emotionally, we will see it most of the time. If you take the time to listen to people, you might be saving a life. You will not push people over edge by asking if they want to hurt themselves.

Chapter Four

Moving Forward

As I stated before, I am not a doctor—and I don't pretend to be one. I didn't research every book or every medical expert to tell you what happened—and still happens—to me. Everything I wrote was based upon my experiences. I might have left out some important passages, quotes, or figures, but please understand what I didn't leave out. I didn't leave out the most important information that saved my spirit, which was learning to communicate with loved ones, friends, therapists, and clergy. I also learned that my department wasn't going to take me off the streets because I was experiencing very normal feelings from a very traumatic event.

By learning how to listen to emotions instead of words, my family was able to tell me that I wasn't lost. I just couldn't hear them trying to help me. With their help, I was able to learn how to be a father, brother, son, grandson, and friend again. In the end, it was okay for me to cry. I am human and not robotic. Over time, I had built walls or barriers to keep people out, and these walls are different from the walls we as police officers have for our personal safety. It's important to be on your toes and keep people out of your sacred space-or the space that can get us hurt or even killed-which is seven feet between you and another.

To be more specific, statistically police officer's get hurt or even killed within five to seven feet of their assailants.

On the other hand, by putting up these walls, we leave so much out. We leave out what makes us all special—our hearts. That was the reason I became a police officer almost thirty years ago. We see and go through so much that we take on an identity that makes us forget that we're human. I lost that identity—but I found it again after plenty of pain, anguish, and love.

In conclusion, please understand that if you or friends ever suffer from a traumatic event, it's okay to cry and talk about it. What's not okay is to think you can handle it on your own. It's not okay to let one drink of alcohol lead to another to mask the pain. It's not okay to have one sleeping pill lead to another because the nightmares keep you awake. These vices manifest into total self-destruction.

It is okay to understand that stress can be anything from gossip to bullying children or bosses. It doesn't take an earthquake, tornado, hurricane, rape, or shooting to have your world become unraveled over a very short period of time. All it takes is letting our feelings control us instead of us controlling them. All it takes is the belief that you can handle it, when it's handling you.

We are people with real feelings from different religions, beliefs, shapes, and sizes, but we all have feelings. If you don't take care of the most important part of your person—your spirit—you may end up writing your own *Prison of Darkness*. I was able to climb out of this darkness by learning to forgive myself and Duran. I forgave myself for the way I had treated my family, and I forgave Duran for the pain he had caused me and my family. In the end, I learned that Duran was just trying to belong in society. I am not making up excuses for his actions, but understanding why he did what he did made it a lot easier to forgive him. Duran had been reminded all his life that he was nobody—and he would never be anybody—until a well-known gang approached him and told him that they would love him and make him feel special. Duran was so dark and desperate to be someone that he was willing to die for it.

I also learned that just before he came to us from the corner store where he retrieved the gun, he met his girlfriend right outside the store. She was pushing her baby in a baby carriage. Duran's last words of kindness were: "I might not have felt special, but I will always make you feel special. Daddy's going to get some money to buy you a dress to be baptized in."

In the end, this forgiveness and unconditional love drove me from the depths of hell into the light of love. There are no excuses for the pain and suffering he caused me—and both of our families. I understand that if I continued to hate Duran and everything he stood for, I would have driven myself over the edge. I'd been told so many times that I was a hero and took on that Identity. Like Superman, I thought I could save the world, when I couldn't save myself. Superman never cried, so why should I? In reality, I was crying inside but couldn't show my weakness. During my presentations about PTSD, it was the participants that showed me that I was human. It was ok to cry. I discovered it wasn't me helping them, but they were helping me. The more I talked about the event, the more I remembered what had been locked in my brain for so long. It was such a release to let go of those horrible memories.

I have come so far since the event and look forward to going even further. I look forward to sharing my experiences with as many people as I can as long as I have oxygen in my lungs. If one person reads this book and learns from it, then I have changed the world in one small way.

It took some time, but life has gone on for me—as it will for you. It took me a while because I didn't have anyone teaching me what I had to go through so painfully. Today, life is different, as I find myself learning to live with PTSD. My children have told me that I am much more patient and less aggressive than I used to be. My son Perry has also told me that I have learned to not judge people for who they are, but what they do. He said, "Dad in the past you used to push people in the right direction, now you guide them."

Some more food for thought: on December 1, 2011, *USA Today* reported that ten thousand soldiers are reporting PTSD every three months to the Department of Veterans Affairs. These are our children, brothers, sisters, aunts, uncles, mothers, and fathers. Now is the time to start learning to listen to each other—and not with our ears, but our hearts.